T0209069

Thoughts to Reflect On

Robert Burns

authorHOUSE®

AuthorHouse™
1663 Liberty Drive
Bloomington, IN 47403
www.authorhouse.com
Phone: 833-262-8899

Published by AuthorHouse 12/20/2022

ISBN: 978-1-6655-7875-2 (sc)
ISBN: 978-1-6655-7873-8 (hc)
ISBN: 978-1-6655-7874-5 (e)

Library of Congress Control Number: 2022923647

Print information available on the last page.

Good Morning, Start today with an open mind and being receptive to new thoughts and ideas. You will be amazed by all of the wonderful and exciting/interesting things that you will become aware of as they unfold for you.

Good Morning, Take a moment or two and look into the mirror, look into your eyes and say "I love you". Say it with emotion and your day will unfold before you as a miracle since you admitted that you love yourself.

Good Morning, Lets focus on the F word today. Forgiveness will free you from living in the past and allow you to soar into your future with a free mind You do not have to say it to the actual person, just say it while seeing them in your mind and say it from your heart.

Good Morning, The most powerful energy in the universe is love. The second most powerful is fear so if you find yourself with fearful thoughts, replace them with loving thoughts. It is not easy however it is doable.

Good Morning, When your eyes are open, you can see alot and yet, when your mind is open, you can and do see so much more, You are allowing the "hidden" things in and suddenly everything begins to make sense.

Good Morning, Did you know that you are either moving forward or moving backward in life, Their is no standing still. Just as time seems to move so quickly, so must we or we will be left behind Now is the real time.

Good Morning, Most of us have developed the habit of looking "out there" for for the answers that we seek whereas if we look within, we will find whatever it is we are seeking as everything we want/seek, is within us. Finding it is the challenge.

Good Morning, Do you really know who you are? Not by job title or profession, Your spirit knows who you are and has the answer so pay close attention to your feelings (heart) and the answer will be made known to you in a reasonable period of time.

Good Morning, Are you aware of the fact that you are completely in charge of your day at all times The magic word is attitude so keep a positive and go forward attitude and go forward and be aware of the miracles that take place all around you, Enjoy it.

Good Morning, What gets you excited? When you are able to determine what it is, you will realize your lifes purpose so follow it and you will be very successful and enjoy the ride, Kife is meant to be joyous and fun.

Good Morning, Let me ask you, are you living your truth or are you living that what you think others are expecting of you and approve of? What gets you enthused as that could very well be your lifes purpose, Now that is something to think about isn't it?

Good Morning, Let me ask you, are you keeping your mind and thoughts open to new and energetic ways of being? If you are, you will experience life in a much more healthy and enlightened way plus you will be a great role model for others.

Good Morning, as you venture out and into your day today, keep reminding yourself just what a miracle you are After doing that, proceed to live that truth which ought to be very easy for you to do, This is not at all EGO, it is simply self appreciation,

Good Morning, As has been said, the most powerful energy in the universe is Love. Start each day by spreading yours to all you come in contact with and ask them to do the same. The world needs it badly so please do your part and God Bless You.

Good Morning, Here is a question for you to answer yourself. Where are you going during this particular lifetime? What are your dreams/goals? I hope they are big dreams and goals since you definitely have the capability of achieving them.

Good Morning, As you proceed into and through your day today and every day, Please be aware that you are very special and you are very much loved. You can share this love with others as you go through each day and soon love will be a dominate way of life. Isn't that what we all desire?

Good Morning, Think about this for a minute or two, Nothing will prevent you from reaching your potential as much as a comfort zone. It is something you do not need to restrict yourself with. You are emotionally strong and very intelligent so move forward and live the life you came here to live.

Good Morning, each and every 24 hour period presents us with yet, another opportunity to both expand our knowledge as well as to realize our ultimate purpose for our life. In other words, the reason we are here and to begin living it.

Good Morning, deep inside you {each of u s} there is an intelligence a power that you may not be completely aware of at the present moment yet. If you trust your feelings and use your focus and energy as you do so, You will become completely aware.,

Good Morning, before you do anything today, please remind yourself just how wonderful you are as well as talented. Know this in both your head and heart, then proceed with your day and spread both good will and positive energy to all you come in contact with.

Good morning, and welcome to another day in which to expand your knowledge and develop trust for your feelings. Life is given to us in order to have many experiences in order to learn from them. There are no mistakes in life, only lessons which will be repeated until learned

Good Ming, Another day in which to grow in knowledge as well as emotional experience. Life is given to us in order to have many experiences in which to grow and learn from. As I have stated, there are no mistakes in life, only lessons.

Good Morning, It is amazing what you become aware of when your mind is open plus what you can see We are constantly surrounded with possibilities and yet when our mind is closed off, we fail to recognize them so open your mind and take advantage of them.

Good Morning, Let me ask you, are you prepared for all of the wonderful things that will take place today? First you must realize that they are all taking place in your mind so that places you and only you in complete charge of the type of day that you have sooo, make it wonderful.

Good Morning, Here is a thought for you to ponder, do you look inside yourself for validation or do you look to others? Your answer will let you know your degree of self confidence that you have for yourself. Always look within as the answers are always within you plus it means you trust yourself.

Good Morning, Another new day, Please remember this, when you have an open and an inquisitive mind, your day will provide you with many enjoyable experiences and you will be able to recognize them so make it a point to enjoy all of these fun times and proceed to allow them to take place often as you are in charge of your days

Good Morning, Do you realize that who you are is so much more valuable than what you are? As you become more aware of this fact, life begins to smooth out and suddenly you view events much differently than you previously did. You view them from the spiritual aspect since that is who you are.

Good Morning, You have before you an extremely wonderful day so let me ask you, Exactly what are you going to do with it? Will you seize the opportunity to expand your knowledge and wisdom? Or will you waste it doing meaningless things in order to "kill" time. As with everything, the choice is yours so make the best one to fit into your life plan.

Good Morning, Here is a question for you. are you a Mind or a Being? The mind is a direct descendent of the EGO whereas a Being is a direct descendent of God. The mind {EGO} is never satisfied and the Being is content and a loving presence. So, which one do you profess to be?

Good Morning, Here is an interesting thought for you to ponder. When you say the words "my body", you are showing ownership and not at all showing being. You are a spirit inhabiting the body that you own and it is not who you are, it is simply the home your spirit is dwelling in this time around. Being spirit, removes any and all limits you may have placed upon yourself.

Good Morning, You are a beautiful, resourceful, and intelligent person. You are also emotionally powerful. Now, being completely aware of these attributes, proceed into your day filled and overjoyed with love for all, including yourself.

Good Morning, Ponder this thought, do you feel that you have to be right in an argument all the time? There is no right or wrong, only judgement and opinions brought on by the EGO. Let me use this bit of information and that is "A an convinced against his will is of the same opinion still". Think on that and avoid arguments.

Good Morning, What ever you send out into the universe is going to come back to you over and over. Send out love and welcome it as it returns to you and this can take place in many ways. After all, like attracts like and you are love in a beautiful package.

Good Morning, Always remember that who you are is a God given miracle and what you are is always found in your mind and the minds of others. Please do not allow your ego to cause you to think less of your self since you are very, very, special.

Good Morning, Please get into the habit of listening to your feeling and pay close attention, They are messages from your heart and always are very truthful.

Good Morning, Please remember that you are a beautiful spirit who is having a human experience. As this becomes your reality, allow yourself to enjoy your day as after all, you are creating it.

Good Morning, This is an interesting thought for you today, What you place in your mind will take you through the day and yet that which you place in your heart, will take you through your whole life. Please be aware of that.

Good Morning, This morning, prior to heading out, look in the mirror, into your eyes and say "I love you", say it at least ten tomes and say it with emotion/feeling. then go about your day knowing you are loved very much.

Good Morning, This morning before you embark on your day, decide to create a remarkable and fantastic experience for both yourself and others with whom you come in contact with As you do this not only will you brighten their day but you will also brighten your day too.

Good Morning, Another great day in which to experience the joys of life while both acquiring knowledge of self as well as others. A great time to learn as much as possible.

Good Morning, Let me ask you, do you feel that you must be right in an argument? EGO is what determines that particular mindset as their are no winners in an argument as stated in an earlier page.

Good morning, This morning break free from the world of attachments as that is the EGO at work. Who you are on the inside is all that is important to not only yourself but to others also. Today you should practice forgiveness and gratitude as they come from spirit.

Good Morning, Here is a brand new day for you to get out there amongst others and start to spread light where there is darkness. Love where there is hate. So smile at the ones who are frowning and send caring to those who do not appear to care about themselves.

Good Morning, As you look back on your life and all that you have accomplished plus all that you have been through, you must be feeling a sense of pride. You now are beginning to realize that you are a very special and unique person so enjoy the feelings as you have earned them.

Good Morning, Today as you look in the mirror, recognize the absolute perfection you see looking back at you. It has always been there as you have been created perfectly. you are perfection.

Good Morning, Keep this in mind. Your body does exactly what your mind tells it to do. Please be certain that it is your mind and not anothers that your body is paying attention to and once you have done that, proceed to create a wonderful day every day and enjoy yourself.

Good Morning, As you open your eyes each and every morning, be sure to open your mind as well. When you do, you begin to see and to know everything that is around you so you can decide just what to focus on each day.

Good morning, Here we are with yet another opportunity to receive even more information to assist us on life's journey. The wisdom {knowledge applied} is needed in order to accomplish what we set out to do when we arrived here so now is another chance.

Good Morning, This is a very special day {as they all are} yet this is the now that we always spend our time in. Not the yesterdays or the tomorrows but the day we are presently in, the NOW so use this time to your own benefit and enjoy.

Good morning, are you aware that when you do the same things over and over on a day by day basis, that you are actually living in the past? Why do that anymore because using the power of your mind, you are perfectly able to create the future of your dreams.

Printed in the United States
by Baker & Taylor Publisher Services